George Rose

A Brief Examination into the Increase of the Revenue,

Commerce And Navigation of Great Britain

George Rose

A Brief Examination into the Increase of the Revenue, Commerce And Navigation of Great Britain

ISBN/EAN: 9783744725668

Printed in Europe, USA, Canada, Australia, Japan

Cover: Foto ©ninafisch / pixelio.de

More available books at **www.hansebooks.com**

A

BRIEF EXAMINATION

INTO THE

INCREASE

OF THE

Revenue, Commerce, and Navigation,

OF

GREAT BRITAIN,

SINCE THE

CONCLUSION OF THE PEACE IN
1 7 8 3.

" *Si palatinas videt æquus Arces,*
" *Remque Romanam, Latiumquè felix,*
" *Alterum in Luſtrum, meliuſque ſemper*
　　　　　　" *Proroget Ævum.*"

THE FOURTH EDITION,

WITH CONSIDERABLE ADDITIONS,

·*LONDON:*

PRINTED FOR JOHN STOCKDALE, PICCADILLY, 1793.

[Price 1 s. 6 d.]

INTRODUCTION.

THE following pamphlet, firſt publiſhed early in the laſt year, was intended to ſhew with fairneſs and accuracy,
the real ſituation of the Country, as to its
Revenue, Commerce, and Navigation; the
utmoſt care was taken to avoid all political
diſcuſſion, and to keep clear of every thing
that had relation to matters of Party; but
even that caution could not enſure univerſally
a candid conſideration of the ſubject; there
are ſome men diſinclined to believe their
Country in a ſtate of encreaſing proſperity,
eſpecially under an adminiſtration they do
not like, and who, with that impreſſion on
their minds, will either refuſe their aſſent to
the cleareſt propoſitions, or will advance
others that cannot be ſupported either by
facts or argument.

The only attempt however to invalidate
the encouraging proſpect reſulting from this
enquiry, which has yet come to the author's
knowledge, was made by a writer in a news-
paper *, who undertook to ſhew that the
Country *has been* in a much better ſituation
than it was in the beginning of 1792; in
order to which he ſtates, that in two of the
years from 1787 to 1790 the Balance of

* Morning Chronicle of May 5th 1792.

A 2   Trade

Trade was againſt us, and that the four years from 1772 to 1775 were more favorable (meaning thereby that the Exports bore a greater proportion to the Imports) than from 1787 to 1790, by no leſs a ſum than £.11,505,000; and then aſſerts, " there " cannot be a clearer propoſition, than that " when the Imports exceed the Exports the " Balance muſt be paid in gold or ſilver;" the ſtatements are from this pamphlet, and are correct as far as they go, but they are partially extracted; the reaſoning upon them is not juſt, and the laſt aſſertion is utterly unfounded as applied to this Country; the Imports in 1787 and 1788, ſays the writer, exceeded the Exports by £.1,491,000, paſſing by entirely the two following years, 1789 and 1790, when the Exports exceeded the Imports by £.2,509,000: Admitting therefore for a moment a compariſon of the Exports and Imports to be a fair criterion of national proſperity, it would have been more candid not to have ſtopped at 1788 to ſhew the ſtate of our Commerce in the beginning of 1792; but that would not have anſwered the intended purpoſe. It is worthy of obſervation too, that in the whole period from 1787 to 1790, the Exportation of

Britiſh

Britifh Goods bore a larger proportion to that of foreign merchandize, than in the one from 1772 to 1775, which is an incontefable proof of the rapid increafe of our manufaċtures.

Another inftance of the writer's candor is his complaining of the *calamitous year* 1772 being included in the firft four years of the comparifon, becaufe he fays in that year, the Eaft India Company poftponed as well as reduced their dividends, and the whole credit of Scotland, and of a great part of the city of London was fhook to its centre.

What effeċts thofe events produced will be feen by the following account, which proves that the Exports in that *calamitous year*, were confiderably higher than in any one of the three that followed, and the Imports much higher than the average of the other three ;—he choofes to compare the year 1771 however, with 1772, becaufe in the former there were immenfe quantities of goods fent to America, in confequence of the Trade being then opened after almoft a total interruption with a great part of that continent for a confiderable length of time, by their non-importation agreement : the following account will af-

§ certain

certain this, and will prove that the years from 1772 to 1775, shew the higheft fair average of the Exports during the laft peace; 1771 could not be included without going back at leaft two years, for the reafons above mentioned.

		Value of Exports.
1768	- - -	£. 16,622,000
1769	- - - -	15,001,000
1770	- - - -	15,995,000
1771	- - - -	18,470,000
1772	- - - -	17,719,000
1773	- - - -	16,531,000
1774	- - - -	17,285,000
1775	- - - -	16,325,000

Average of thefe 8 years £. 16,743,000, which is nearly £. 1,000,000 lefs than the Exports in the year which the writer felected as a calamitous one.

It will not, however, be acknowledged, that it is highly difadvantageous to a Country to import to a greater extent than it exports; a different opinion prevails, and a late writer, for whofe inimitable talents the beft informed men have the higheft refpect, is no mean authority on the fubject.

"* This Balance of Produce and Con-

* Smith's Wealth of Nations, Vol. iii. ch. 3. p. 251.

" fumption

" fumption is entirely different from what
" is called the Balance of Trade. It might
" take place in a Nation which had no fo-
" reign Trade, but which was entirely fe-
" parated from all the world. It may take
" place in the whole globe of the earth,
" of which the Wealth, Population, and
" Improvement may be either gradually in-
" creafing or gradually decaying."

" The Balance of Produce and Confump-
" tion may be conftantly in favour of a Na-
" tion, though what is called the Balance
" of Trade be generally againft it. A Na-
" tion may import to a greater value than
" it exports for half a century, perhaps, to-
" gether ; the Gold and Silver which comes
" into it during all this time, may be all
" immediately fent out of it ; its circulating
" Coin may gradually decay, different forts
" of Paper Money being fubftituted in its
" place, and even the Debts too, which it
" contracts in the principal Nations with
" whom it deals, may be gradually increaf-
" ing, and yet its real wealth, the unchange-
" able value of the annual produce of its
" Lands and Labour, may, during the fame
" period, have been increafing in a much
" greater proportion. The ftate of our
" North American Colonies, and of the
. " Trade

INTRODUCTION.

" Trade which they carried on with Great
" Britain, before the commencement of the
" difturbances in 1775, may ferve as a proof
" that this is by no means an impoffible
" fuppofition."

It cannot, however, be neceffary to pur-
fue the difcuffion further, as our Exports
have for four years paft exceeded our Imports; and becaufe in any event, as to
Great Britain, *the affertion* is ridiculous in
the extreme, when it is confidered, that
of the value of our Imports nearly a * fifth
part on an average is from our Colonies in
the Weft Indies, a very large proportion of
which is fpent in this country, and confe-
quently contributes to the increafe of our in-
land as well as our cuftoms Revenue; a large
proportion too of thofe from the Eaft Indies, affords the means of remittance to the
Company of their Territorial Revenues, and
to individuals, of their private fortunes †.
The Balance of Trade muft therefore be infinitely more againft us than it has yet been,

---

* Average Annual Value of Imports into Great Britain
for five years, 1787, to 1792 £. 18,450,200
Ditto . . from the Weft Indies - - - 3,836,600

† Average Annual Value of Imports from the Eaft Indies,
from 1768 to 1775 - - - £. 1,760,000.
Ditto - - - - 1787 to 1792 - - - - 3,457,000.

before

before we are *thereby* compelled to fend out Gold and Silver, efpecially when the growing profperity of our fifheries is confidered *.
Bullion has been and always will be fent to fome countries, in the general courfe of Trade, while we are importing it from others.

After thefe obfervations, it is hardly neceffary to add, that the Imports have been greatly. fwelled, in feveral inftances, for fome years paft, by an increafed demand of Raw Materials for our Manufactures; in the article of Cotton Wool, the average annual excefs of the laft four years, compared with the period of 1768 to 1775, is 23,000,000 lbs. †

The rapid increafe of our Commerce, Navigation, and Manufactures, in the courfe of the year fince the publication of the firft edition of this Enquiry, has exceeded the moft fanguine expectations on the fubject, as will be fhewn in the following fheets: The advantages refulting from thence have however fuffered an interruption from a

* Average Annual Value of Oil imported into Great Britain from our Fifheries, from 1768 to 1775 - £. 23,694
Ditto - - - - - - - - - 1787 to 1792 - - 206,480
† At 2s. per lb. is worth £. 2,300,000.

concurrence

concurrence of temporary circumftances, very little connected with the war with France; it would be extremely difficult to afcertain to what extent the demand for our Manufactures is leffened by the difturbances prevailing on the continent of Europe, but the only immediate confequence in that refpect of the hoftilities in which we are engaged, is the excluding us from Exports to the French dominions, to the value of £. 717,000 per Annum, on an average, fince the Commercial Treaty, which is lefs than half of the Increafe of the Value of our Manufactures exported in the laft year above the preceding one. Commercial Credit may be affected by various caufes independently of War; it was in periods of Peace, and apparently of the higheft National Profperity, that Holland, in the year 1762 or 1763, and England in 1772, fuffered great inconvenience for a fhort time from a Want of Credit; the exertions now made for relief of the Mercantile and Manufacturing Interefts are confiderable, and will, it is trufted, extricate the Country from its diftrefs effectually: Confidence among Merchants and Traders was wanting more than Money, and the means for

reftoring

reftoring that, appear likely to attain the object fo much to be wifhed for. In forming a judgment in what degree the full effects of the growing Profperity of the Country may be checked by the prefent War, it fhould be confidered that we have not now, as in the laft inftance, half the world againft us, but have to contend with one nation only, already engaged in hoftilities with a great part of Europe, and that we fhall not be again reftrained in deftroying the Commerce, and preventing the Supplies of our Enemy, by neutral Powers infifting on their right of being carriers.

The following ftate of our Trade during the war of 1756, will indeed afford a reafonable expectation, that our Commerce and Manufactures may not be materially affected by that caufe now; the Revenue, independent of new Taxes, muft in a great degree have kept pace with our Imports, which are here fhewn: A fimilar account during the laft war, would in no degree enable a juft comparifon, becaufe during that, the whole Trade with the colonies which now form the American States was entirely interrupted, and we loft moft of our Weft India iflands.

An

An ACCOUNT of IMPORTS.

	Exclufive of new Colonies.	From new Colonies.	Prize Goods,	TOTAL
1755	£.8,722,000	—	—	£.8,722,0
1756	7,750,000	—	£.211,266	7,961,2
1757	8,200,000	—	627,553	8,827,5
1758	7,787,000	—	1,052,522	8,839,5
1759	8,408,000	£.72,726	441,364	8,922,0
1760	8,942,000	426,521	465,602	9,834,1
1761	8,799,000	496,194	248,702	9,543,8
1762	7,733,000	833,749	302,819	8,869,5
1763	10,471,000	—	—	10,471,0

An ACCOUNT of EXPORTS.

Exclusive of new Colonies.	To new Colonies.	Prize Goods.	TOTAL.
£.11,065,000	—	—	£.11,065,000
11,446,000	—	£.274,545	11,720,545
11,132,000	—	901,207	12,033,207
11,717,000	—	1,205,809	12,922,809
13,211,000	£. 43,339	692,743	13,947,082
14,234,000	165,199	340,336	14,739,535
14,319,000	358,235	195,164	14,872,499
12,708,000	601,678	235,364	13,545,042
14,106,000	—	—	14,106,000

A BRIEF

A

BRIEF EXAMINATION, &c.

THE immenfe accumulation of the Public Debts, and the depreffed ftate of Public Credit, of the Revenue, and of the Funds, at the clofe of the laft War, together with the lofs of feveral extenfive and populous Colonies in North America, led fome of the ableft and moft experienced men in the Kingdom, not in general inclined to defpondency, to doubt whether it would be poffible for Great Britain, reduced apparently to the loweft ebb by a fucceffion of misfortunes, and by expences unprecedented in any former time, ever to regain Profperity at home or Influence abroad. The events, however, which have fince happened, fhew as well the effect which may be produced by a refolution to encounter the difficulties of the moft embarraffed fituation, as the extent of the refources to

3   be

be derived from a spirit of national Industry and Enterprize.

The Object of the following Statement is to direct the attention of the Public to the present circumstances of the Country, with respect to its Finances and Commerce, compared with the period above alluded to, as an inducement to perseverance in the same laudable exertions; and at the same time to bring to recollection some of the principal measures which have contributed essentially to the restoration of our Credit, and to the increase of our Wealth and Trade.

It would be foreign to our Purpose to trace the several ministerial changes which took place towards the close of the War, and upon the Pacification; it is sufficient to remark, that the definitive treaty of Peace was signed in September 1783, and that the present Administration commenced at the close of the year; a memorable political struggle then prevailed during several months, and it was not till after the meeting of the

new

new Parliament, in the fpring of 1784, that the Government was in a fituation to propofe efficient meafures refpecting the Revenues of the country.

The produce of the Permanent Taxes for a year, to 5th January 1784, had been £. 9,667,206, to which fhould be added £. 527,053 for duties due by the Eaft India Company within the year, but not paid till a future one, making in the whole £. 10,194,259; at this period the intereft of the funded debt alone was £. 8,000,284, befides which there were outftanding Demands fatisfied in 1784, by a loan of £. 6,000,000; thefe, together with Navy and Victualling Bills, and Ordnance Debentures, amounted in the whole to TWENTY-SEVEN MILLIONS, (exclufive of * £. 2,000,000 afterwards granted by par-

Amount of Revenue in 1783 and of the Charges upon it.

* This might very properly be confidered as a part of the Unfunded debt; becaufe the claim on the generofity of the country, to whatever extent it was thought proper to admit it, exifted at the conclufion of the war, although it was not liquidated till fome time after;—but it is omitted here, as the profits of the Lottery have been applied to the payment of it.

C   liament

liament to the American Sufferers) and were
funded in 1784 and 1785.

The new funds thus created, increafed the annual intereſt of the Debt to
£.9,275,000; to which muſt be added
£. 260,000 for the annual intereſt of Exchequer bills, and £. 1,048,000 for the
annual charges on the Aggregate Fund (including the Civil Liſt) and the amount of
Duties appropriated for particular purpoſes
and not applicable to the national Expenditure.

The reſult is, that the whole charges on
the Revenue, excluſive of all the Eſtabliſhments, amounted to £.10,575,000; which
exceeded the produce of the Permanent
Taxes to January 5th 1784, by £.380,741.
It was certainly reaſonable to expect ſome
Increaſe of Revenue from the reſtoration
of Peace, but ſuch Increaſe could not at
that time be depended upon with certainty;
the only exiſting Reſources for ſupplying
the deficiency of the Permanent Revenue,
and for defraying the expences of all the
annual Eſtabliſhments (which could by no

2   calculation

calculation be fuppofed to be lefs than £.4,000,000, and have in fact proved to be more) were the Duties on Land and Malt, producing on an Average about £.2,560,000, which left a deficiency, on the whole, of ONE MILLION EIGHT HUNDRED AND TWENTY THOUSAND POUNDS, below the Sums neceffary to provide for the annual expences, exclufive of any provifion for the reduction of the National Debt,

Of all the Circumftances in this fituation, none operated in more ways to deprefs the Public Credit, and encreafe its embarraffments, than the large amount of the Unfunded Debt before ftated; yet this very depreffion of Credit added to the difficulty of removing the Evil,

The £.3 Per Cents, which at the Peace of 1763 rofe to £.95, did not on the late Peace rife higher than £.69, at which price they were in March 1783, but they continued fo high only a few weeks; they afterwards fell gradually till February 1784,

when

when they were at £. 55 and a fraction ; and were in May and June 1784 (when the Debt was funded) at £. 58 *.

Deficien-
cies of
Taxes dur-
ing the
War, and
in 1783.
The Account given by the Committee of Finance in 1782, throws a further light on thefe difcouraging profpects, and particularly on the deficiency of new Taxes impofed during the War, compared with the increafed Intereft on the Money then borrowed. It appears by that Report, that there was an accumulated Deficiency of £. 2,246,000 of the Intereft of Monies raifed between 1776 and 1782, and an annual one of £. 395,931.

* They fell in a few months to £. 54⅛, in confequence of the large Loan and heavy Taxes of this feffion, and did not rife again to £. 58 till July 1785. They were in February 1782 as low as £. 53¾. In the war of 1744, they were only 5 months under £. 80, the loweft during the rebellion in 1746 £. 74¼; and at the Peace which followed, they rofe above par. They then fell in a few months to £. 99 and £. 98; but between 1750 and 1756, they varied from £. 100 to 105½ (once rifing to £. 106) except during a few months in 1751, when they were from £. 97 to £. 99. From 1765 to 1776 they fluctuated principally from £. 87 to £. 92 or £. 93; in one week rifing to £. 94. On the 30th of April 1793, in a time of war, and under circumftances diftreffing to the Credit of the Country, they were £. 77⅜.

The

The ground of Defpondency indeed increafed at the commencement of the Peace, when better Expectations were naturally entertained; for the Taxes of 1783, which were impofed to pay an Intereft of more than £. 560,000, did not produce half that Sum.

It appears further, by the fame Report, that the Annual Amount of all the Taxes, including the old and the new, from 1774 to 1782, from Eafter to Eafter, was as under,

Amount of Permanent Taxes from 1774 to 1782.

1774 to 1775	- - £. 8,439,000
1775 to 1776	- - - 8,068,000
1776 to 1777	- - - 8,047,000
1777 to 1778	- - - 8,782,000
1778 to 1779	- - - 7,967,000
1779 to 1780	- - - 8,747,000
1780 to 1781	- - - 10,289,000
1781 to 1782	- - - 9,245,000*;

* To which fhould be added £. 163,000 for duties due by the Eaft India Company within the year, which were not paid till a fubfequent one.

and

and in the year ending January 5th, 1784, the Taxes amounted to £. 10,194,259, including some Duties due by the East India Company in that year, but not paid till a subsequent one.

Increase of the Interest of the Debt during the War beyond Increase of Revenue.
The whole Permanent Revenue therefore was £. 1,755,259 higher in 1783, than in 1774, and the Interest of the Debt funded and to be funded was increased £. 4,864,000, so that the total increase of Revenue was less than the increase of annual Interest by THREE MILLIONS ONE HUNDRED AND EIGHT THOUSAND POUNDS.

It is not easy for the Mind of Man to conceive a Task more painful than the Attempt to provide for great Exigencies, in such a situation as has been described; fortunately however, although there was in general little hope of success, there appeared a spirit in all ranks of people, to support any exertion which might afford a chance of extricating the Country from its difficulties.

The

_ The whole of the Navy and Victualling Bills, and Ordnance Debentures, were funded in the two firft Seffions of the new Parliament, for the Intereft of which efficient Taxes were provided; and from this time a fyftem of Meafures was adopted and purfued, not only to impofe fuch new Taxes as might be neceffary, but alfo to enforce and improve the collection of exifting Duties, in order to equalize the Public Income to the Expenditure, and farther to produce a Surplus applicable to the reduction of the Debt. Debt funded and Taxes impofed fince the Peace.

The Taxes impofed in 1784 and 1785, produced in 1786, £. 938,000, and thofe in 1789, more than £. 60,000 *.

With a view to the improvement of the Revenue by Regulations, an Act, containing feveral provifions againft Smuggling, was paffed in the firft Seffion; which had Smuggling Act.

* Thefe laft were impofed to pay the Intereft of the Loan of £. 1,000,000 raifed by way of Tontine, to defray extraordinary Expences fince the Peace.

an immediate effect, in confiderably leſſening
the illicit Trade carried on in Cutters, and
other fmall Veſſels, all round the Coaſts of
this Kingdom; the Act extended the hover-
ing Laws, reſtrained the built and rigging
of the Veſſels, prohibited their being armed,
and directed the deſtroying fuch as ſhould
be taken, that they might not be again uſed
by the Smugglers: The operation of this
Law was however greatly aided by another,
generally known by the name of the Commutation Act, which reduced the Duties on
Tea fo low, as to prevent the fraudulent Importer from carrying on any profitable
traffic in that Commodity. . It is impoſſible
to calculate the exact Increaſe which theſe
Meaſures occaſioned in other branches of the
Revenue; but it is evident, that the de-
priving the Smuggler of the principal Article
in the aſſortment of his Cargo, muſt have
produced a great effect. The benefits of
the Commutation Act in other points of
view fall under a feparate confideration; but
it is proper to obſerve here, that the gradual
diminution of Smuggling ever fince, is the
beſt

**Commuta-
tion Act.**

beſt proof of the efficacy of this and the other Meaſures which have been adopted.

In 1786 the Manifeſt Act was paſſed; which has nearly annihilated a branch of Smuggling, carried on formerly to a certain extent, from regular trading Ships on their arrival in the river Thames, and at the ſeveral Ports of the Kingdom, and has conſiderably corrected the Frauds in the obtaining Bounties and Drawbacks.

Manifeſt Act.

In the ſame year the meaſure of exciſing Wine was adopted; the benefits reſulting from which will be made moſt evident, by ſhewing the increaſed legal Conſumption, and the benefit derived to the Revenue therefrom:

Exciſing Wine.

D

Quantities

	Tons.	Duty after deducting Drawbacks.
Quantities imported in 1790 - - -	29,189	£. 804,167
1791 - - -	33,092	- - - 910,920
1792 - - -	35,525	- - - 1,031,704
	97,806	2,746,791
Average of the three last years - -	32,602	915,597
Average of 1784, 1785, and 1786 -	15,953	625,454
Average Increase - - - Tons	16,649	£. 290,143

The

The increase of Revenue, when the comparative Quantities are confidered, would have been much greater, but for the reduction of Duties adopted for the purpofe of obtaining great commercial Advantages by the Treaty of Commerce with France, which had been figned on the 26th of September 1786.

Portugal Wines were reduced one-third, and French Wines one-half.

The Revenue derived a further advantage from the Confolidation of the Cuftoms in 1787; a part of this arofe from converting the fractional parts of the Rates into Integers, which, though lowered in a few inftances, were raifed in more, and had, upon the whole, the effect of producing fome Increafe *. Much more, however, was gained by a judicious lowering of the Duties on Drugs and a few other articles, the confumption of which was before fupplied by the Smuggler.

Confolidation of the Cuftoms.

* In 1788, £. 20,853.—In 1789, £. 22,696.—In 1790, £. 24,292.—In 1791, £. 25,340.—In 1792, £. 25,930.

The

The additional Rates on fome forts of Wood, and the new defcriptions of others for better afcertaining the proper Duties, occafioned likewife an Increafe *.

The Treaty of Commerce with France being carried into effect by this Bill, as to Duties on Importation from that Country, the Revenue of Cuftoms alfo profited, to a fmall extent †, by the Duty impofed on Cambrics, the Rate of which had been ftipulated by the Article of the Treaty which provided for their admiffion into this Kingdom. This gain to the Revenue was obtained without being a detriment to any of our Manufactures, for the fevereft Laws had not been able to prevent the Introduction and ufe of the article ; the Smuggler therefore alone profited by the Prohibition while it exifted. But the moft evident Augmentation of Revenue in con-

Duties on Spirits lowered.

* Thefe amounted on the whole as follows:—In 1788, to £. 43,699.—In 1789, to £. 37,668.—In 1790, to £. 48,697. In 1791, to £. 48,320.—And in 1792, to £. 49,504.

† The Duty amounted in 1790 to near £. 12,000.—In 1791 to £. 13,737.—And in 1792 to £. 10,305.

fequence

fequence of this Act, has arifen from the increafed legal confumption of foreign and Britifh Spirits produced by a confiderable abatement of the Rates; the Duty on Rum and on Britifh Spirits had been fomewhat reduced in 1784, but the great reduction was made by this Law; the effect will appear by the following Accounts:

Produce of the Duties of Excife and Cuftoms on foreign Spirits, exclufive of the additional Duties impofed in 1790–1, in Great Britain, in 1789 - - - - - - - - - - - - £. 948,226

	£.
1790 - - - - - - - - - -	1,082,264 *
1791 - - - - - - - - - -	810,585
1792 - - - - - - - - - -	965,466
	3,806,541

Average of the laft four years - £.951,635

Add the Average Amount of the Duty on Licences to retail Spirits, impofed in order to make good in part the Reduction of the Duties in 1787 - - - - - - - - - - 87,775

Produce of - - - 1784 - - - - - - - - - 1,039,410
560,846

Increafe - - - - - - - - - - 478,564

On

* The high Amount of the Duties in this year, and the Deficiency in the next, was occafioned by the Dealers in Rum taking out all their Stocks in the Bonded Warehoufes, and entering a few Cargoes of Brandy from the neighbouring Ports in France, previous to the Commencement of the new Duties in

On a comparifon of the Duties on Britifh Spirits, it will be feen that there is an
increafe of more than £. 200,000 *.

Average of Duties 1790 to	
1792 inclufive - - -	£.637,778
Amount of Ditto in 1786 - -	430,000
Increafe - - - -	£. 207,778

The notorious evafion of the Tax on Poft
Horfes led to an attempt for the correction
of thofe Frauds, by letting the Duties to
Farm; and the Meafure has procured an annual average Increafe of £.35,000 on the
former Revenue of £.146,000.

Tax on Poft Horfes farmed.

* The additional Duties impofed on Foreign and Britifh
Spirits in the years 1779, 1780, 1781, 1782, on the credit
of which large Sums were lent to the Public, had the effect
each year of confiderably diminifhing the whole produce on
thofe articles,

The

There remained another important Article, of which the Smuggler was fuppofed to furnifh a large proportion, and which (even after he had been driven from the traffic in Tea, and his profits in Spirits had been confiderably reduced) principally enabled him to affort his Cargo with fome advantage ; attempts had been made to prevent the fraudulent trade in Tobacco, by different Acts of Parliament in 1784, and the two following years, without any material fuccefs ; it was therefore thought expedient, in 1789, to apply the fame remedy that had been tried in the cafe of Wine.

The benefits to be expected from this Meafure, did not however protect it from an active though ineffectual refiftance. The great extent of Frauds indeed prevailing, and the evident propriety of collecting as great a Revenue upon the Article as it would bear, furnifhed the ftrongeft reafons for bringing it under the regulations of the Excife;—they were clearly as applicable to the Tobacco Trade as to the others in which they had been found fuccefsful, and

3

the

the number of additional Perfons hereby
fubjected to thefe laws is fmall in comparifon to the object *.

Experience has fhewn the wifdom and
expediency of the Meafure with refpect to
the Revenue; and the Trade, at leaft the
Fair Trade, inftead of fuffering, has been
confiderably extended.

Average Amount of Duties in
   3 Years, ending Michael-
   mas 1792 - - - - - £.578,015
Average Amount of Duties in
   3 Years, ending Michael-
   mas 1789 - - - - - 423,711

£.154,304

---

* The number of manufacturers who were to be fubjected to the Excife Survey by the Bill was 337 : The retail dealers were in general fubject to furvey before, by
felling Tea or other excifeable articles.

E   What

Increafe of
Revenue
from 1783
to 1791.

.What has been the total Improvement of the Revenue from the year 1783 to the prefent time, will appear from the following Statement:

Produce of all the PERMANENT TAXES.

From 5th January 1783 to 5th January 1784		*10,194,259
1784 to	- - 1785 - -	10,856,996
1785 to	- - 1786 - -	†12,104,798
1786 to	- - 1787 - -	‡11,867,055
1787 to	- - 1788 - -	12,923,134
1788 to	- - 1789 - -	13,007,642
1789 to	- - 1790 - -	13,433,068
1790 to	- - 1791 - -	||14,072,978
1791 to	- - 1792 - -	14,132,000
1792 to	- - 1793 - -	14,284,295

* The actual Payments into the Exchequer in this year were £.523,053 less than this sum; but it is added here, as Duties of Customs to that amount, due by the East India Company, were postponed.

† Deducting £.401,118 Duties of Customs paid by the East India Company within this year, which became due in a former one.

‡ Deducting £.522,500 of ditto.

£.233,098 of Custom Duties due by the East India Company had been suspended in 1789.

|| From this Sum should be deducted £.193,000, being the Amount of a 53rd Weekly Payment, which would leave the Produce of the Year £.13,879,000.

E 2

The

The firſt remark which here preſents itſelf is, that the Revenue has almoſt gradually riſen, in the courſe of the laſt ten years,
from £.10,194,259 to £.14,284,295. Of
this great Increaſe, amounting to more than
FOUR MILLIONS, £.1,084,041 * may
be placed to the account of new Taxes impoſed within the period. £.1,165,789 †
has been ſhewn to be derived from the im-
proved collection of ſeveral principal Duties;

* Taxes of 1784 and 1785 • • £.938,000
Conſolidation Act, including Duties on ⎱
  Wood and Cambric, on a medium ⎰ 86,041
  of the three laſt years - - -
Taxes of 1789 • • • • - 60,000

                        £.1,084,041

The Licence Duties on Dealers in Spirituous Liquors are
not included in the above, as thoſe Duties were ſtated to be
impoſed in order to compenſate for the reduction of the Duties on Spirits.

† Foreign Spirits - - - - - £. 478,564
  Britiſh Ditto - - - - -   207,778
  Tobacco - - - - - - -   154,304
  Poſt-Horſe Duty - - - - -   35,000
  Wine - - - - - - -   290,143

                        £.1,165,789

a further

a further Proportion is owing to the Meafures for preventing contraband Trade, and
for the better collection of the Revenues;
and the remainder is to be afcribed to the
Ingenuity and Energy of our Manufacturers,
the Enterprize of our Merchants, and to
the general fpirit of the Nation, which
availed itfelf with fuch efficiency of the ad-.
vantages and bleffings of Peace.

Encouraging as this remarkably flourifh-
ing ftate of the Income of the Country. is,
on the firft view of it, it becomes infinitely
more fo, when we confider that the permanent Taxes have been thus productive, notwithftanding the impofition of temporary
Duties, eftimated at £.800,000 a year, but
producing more, which are not included in
the preceding Statement, as they are appropriated to pay the expences incurred for the Spa-
nifh armament without Funding. An atten-
tive inveftigation of this fubject induced the
Parliament in 1792, proceeding with great
caution, and after providing for various extraordinary Services to a very confiderable

2   amount,

amount, to repeal Taxes which bore hardeft
on the middle and lower claffes of People,
to the extent of more than £. 220,000 a
year; under an impreffion, on no light
ground, that the repeal of the Taxes would
not ftop here. Nothing could be more
honourable to the Parliament, or more encouraging to the Country, than this meafure; becaufe it proved, that although heavy
Taxes were impofed when that was indif-
penfably neceffary for the credit and welfare
of the Nation, yet that there was a difpofi-
tion to lighten the Burdens of the People,
with as little delay as was confiftent with the
real intereft of the Public.

Surplus for
Reduction
of the Na-
tional Debt.
The Meafures thus far defcribed, had
immediate relation to the Increafe of the
Revenue, and it was not thought advifable
to interrupt the Account of them with
referring to any others; but after the preceding Statement, it is impoffible not to
take notice of the moft important of all
the Acts paffed during the period in quef-
tion.

THE

The National Debt

In 1755, previous to the French War, was - - £.72,289,000; the Interest £.2,654,000

In January 1776, before the American War, it was - £. 123,964,000; ditto £.4,411,000

In 1786, previous to which the whole Debt of the laft War was not funded, it was - £.239,154,000 *; ditto £.9,275,000

* Exclufive of a Capital of £.1,991,000 granted by Parliament to Loyalifts, as a Compenfation for Lofs of property in America,

No

No permanent Provifion had ever been made for the progreffive and certain Reduction of it: the Surpluffes of the feveral Funds were indeed directed, by Acts of 3d and 5th Geo. I. to be formed into a Sinking Fund, for the purpofe of reducing the National Debt, but no care was taken to *fecure* the application of thofe Surpluffes; and fome of them were diverted, by fubfequent Acts, to other Purpofes, during the fame Adminiftration in which the Sinking Fund was eftablifhed.

A general opinion is faid to have prevailed, that the public Credit would be effentially injured, (if no worfe confequences fhould follow) whenever the Debt fhould amount to £.100,000,000; and yet, during the Peace which intervened from 1748 to 1755, no Exertions appear to have been made to avert the Evil: in that period no more than £.2,730,000 was paid off. The fame want of Exertion feems to have prevailed again in the following Peace, between 1763 and 1775, as the Debt was in that interval reduced fomething lefs than £. 5,600,000,

The

The neglect, however, of providing formerly an *unalienable* Surplus for the Reduction of the National Debt, when the Country was under fewer Preffures, was not confidered by the Parliament of 1786 as an excufe, notwithftanding all the Difficulties which have been ftated, for withholding from public view the magnitude of the Object; that Parliament had the wifdom and the firmnefs to pafs an Act for vefting, unalienably, in Commiffioners, the Sum of £. 1,000,000 annually; in which every poffible precaution was taken, that could be devifed, for preventing the Surplus from being diverted at any future time, and for carrying to the Account of the Commiffinoers for the purpofes of the Act, the Intereft of fuch Stock as fhould be purchafed, and fuch temporary Annuities as fhould fall in *.

To this great and important object, as well as to the repeal of Taxes, the parlia-

* It may reafonably be attributed in fome degree to this Meafure, that the £. 3 Per Cents. were at the beginning of the laft year as high as they were in the former Peace, when the Intereft of the Debt was lefs than half the prefent Amount; and that they are now, in the month of April 1793, in time of war, much higher than at the end of 1785 and beginning of 1786, after three years of peace.

F   ment

ment of 1792 directed its serious attention; and £. 400,000 was granted out of the Supply of that year to the Commissioners, to be applied by them, over and above the accumulated Annual Sum; with an Expectation arising from an Estimate founded on an Average of four years Produce of the Revenue, that a Sum equal to the Amount of the Taxes repealed might in future be appropriated annually as a permanent addition to the Fund for the Reduction of the National Debt.

Amount of Debt paid off.

Under these provisions, TEN MILLIONS ONE HUNDRED AND NINE THOUSAND FOUR HUNDRED POUNDS of the Capital of the Debt has been purchased * ; and the Amount of the annual Sum applicable this year for the Reduction of it, is ONE MILLION, SIX HUNDRED SIXTY-NINE THOUSAND, FIVE HUNDRED AND EIGHTY-TWO POUNDS, exclusive of the expected annual Addition above suggested.

* And Loyalists Debentures have been satisfied to the Amount of £. 1,444,000, which may be considered as a further Reduction of the Public Debt to that Amount.

The

The attention to the Public Credit did not confine itſelf merely to this Meaſure, for the poſitive Decreaſe of the then exiſting Debt;—notwithſtanding the many extraordinary Expences which a concurrence of Circumſtances produced during the laſt eight years, beyond the ordinary Charges of the Peace Eſtabliſhment, no addition was made to it, except £. 1,000,000 by the Tontine in 1789, and a Navy Debt to the Amount of £.457,950;—deducting therefore theſe Sums from the Amount before ſtated to be paid off, the Debt was diminiſhed at the beginning of the preſent year by £. 8,651,450.

A freſh and ſtriking Inſtance of the determined adherence to the Plan for reducing the Debt, appeared on the Occaſion of the Expences incurred by the threatened rupture with Spain;—the Amount of thoſe was upwards of £. 3,000,000, which Sum was provided for (without making any permanent addition to the National Debt) by impoſing, for a limited time, higher Taxes than had ever been laid on in any year dur-

Extraordinary Expences paid without increaſing the Debt.

F 2   ing

ing a War, fufficient to liquidate the whole within the fpace of four years.

Nothing can more clearly evince the Profperity of the Country, than the fuccefs of this Meafure, without affecting the Produce of any of the old Duties. The Precedent is a moft important one, efpecially as no attempt of the kind had been made fince the commencement of a Public Debt.

Its good Effects are not indeed confined to domeftic Confiderations; fo unequivocal a Proof of National Profperity, and of a Spirit to meet exigencies when they arife, without breaking unneceffarily in upon the fyftem of the Reduction of the Debt, muft contribute to make us refpected by furrounding Nations.

HAVING

HAVING thus shewn the State of the Revenue, and the Diminution of the National Debt, we are naturally led to consider such other Measures, adopted since the meeting of the Parliament in 1784, as have contributed to our present Prosperity; and to close these Remarks with a Comparative Statement of our Trade and Navigation: The Result will demonstrate, that the measures taken for the Improvement of the Revenue, have not prevented a rapid Increase of the Commerce or the Manufactures of the Country; from whence we may also derive some confidence, that that Improvement is neither forced nor accidental.

In stating Causes of Increase to the Revenue, notice was taken of the Commutation Act, passed in 1784; but it remains to shew what Advantages have been derived from it in a Commercial View, as having increased the Importation of Teas by the English East India Company, as under *.

Commercial benefits derived from the Commutation Act.

Average

---

* The quantities actually sold by the East India Company, on the average of 8 Years, from September 1784, to September

Average annual importation by
the Company and their Offi- ℔
cers in 6 years, from 1787 to
1792 inclufive, was - - - 18,108,533
Average of D° for 12 years, 1773
to 1784, both inclufive * - 5,605,074

Increafed Importation - ℔ 12,503,459

The reverfe of this, with refpect to the
quantities of Teas imported into other
Countries, which ufed principally to fupply
our Confumption, is not lefs remarkable;
they have decreafed in proportion as our
Importation has increafed.

The Advantages of fuch a large additional
Importation by the Company, to the Ma-

tember 1792, was lbs. 16,352,423; of which lbs. 2,061,842
were exported, and lbs. 14,290,581 were ufed for Home
confumption.

* The years 1785 and 1786 are omitted in thefe Averages,
becaufe the Act paffed late in 1784, and had only a partial
operation in the two following Years, during which great
Quantities of Tea were bought by the Company in Europe,
for the fupply of this Country.

nufactures,

nufactures, Shipping, and Navigation of this
Country, are obvious; as it either finds a
Market for the Produce of the Company's
Poffeffions in India, or furnifhes a Return
for the Exports of Manufactures from
hence.

The value of Britifh Goods fent to China,
which was in 1782–3 only £.106,000, and
in 1783-4, £.120,000, was in the year
1792, £.626,000; and the average tonnage
of Ships arrived from China in 8 years, from
1776 to 1783 inclufive, was 6,059 annually,
which in 6 years, from 1787 to 1792, was
17,981 annually *.

The Act for regulating the Affairs of the
Eaft India Company, which paffed in the
fame Seffion, 1784, occafioned long and fre-
quent Debates, on certain conftitutional
Points which do not relate to our fubject:
But the effect produced by the fyftem of
management adopted in confequence of it
is no longer equivocal; the Company are

Eaft India
Regulating
Act.

* The Builders meafurement is not to be obtained of all
the fhips previous to 1776.

enabled,

enabled, after a long and expenfive War, to increafe the Dividend to the Proprietors, to make an ample provifion for the reduction of their Debt abroad and at home, to contribute largely to the Public Income, and to make a provifion againft future Calamities: India Stock, which in 1783, in profound Peace, was at £.119, is in April 1793, in time of War, at £.214.

Commercial advantages from excifing Wine.

The meafure of excifing Wine has alfo proved of advantage to the Commerce of the Country, as well as to its Revenue, by occafioning the employment of many additional Ships, chiefly Britifh, in foreign voyages to Spain, Portugal, &c. for the importation of an article, much of which. ufed either to be manufactured at Home, or to be brought over from Guernfey, or the oppofite Coafts of Normandy and Picardy *.

The chief Objections, which at the time were ftated to the excifing Wine and To-

---

* The Quantity is more than double what it was before the Meafure took place. Vide P. 26.

bacco,

[49]

bacco, were founded on the fuppofition of the hardfhips it would bring on the traders in thefe Articles, or of the danger which it might produce to the Conftitution. The firft of thefe Objections has been already taken notice of *; and, with refpect to the fecond, it may be fufficient to remark, that there are now 441 Officers fewer than there were previous to excifing Wine and Tobacco, with Salaries reduced upon the whole in the fum of £.6,900 a year †; this is owing to a reduction of the number in 1787, at which time the Salaries of all the inferior Officers were increafed, in order to remove the ftrong temptation to corruption which they were under before, and to fecure confiderable benefit as well to the Revenue as to the fair trader.

Number of Excife Officers, reduced fince 1784.

* It is remarkable, that fince the excifing thefe two Articles there have been only nine Suits in the Exchequer refpecting them.

† A net revenue of more than £.8,000,000 is now managed at a lefs expence to the Public, and with confiderably fewer Officers, than a revenue much under £.6,000,000 was in 1784.

G   The

Advantages of the Confolidation Act.

The advantages of the Confolidation Act, are in like manner not confined to the Revenue; the Merchants, Traders, and Manufacturers find great Relief from it. The Duties of Cuftoms, which were before fo intricate that few Men in the Country were capable of computing them, are now fo plain, that every Importer can make his own Entries with eafe, and afcertain correctly the amount of what is due on his goods.

Provifion againft future unproductive Taxes.

The Act alfo guards (as far as the nature of the fubject permits) againft the ferious Inconvenience of not providing Productive Taxes to pay the Intereft of Loans in future, by directing the Produce of all new Impofitions, and the Amount of fuch Intereft, to be laid before Parliament at the beginning of each Seffion; for the neceffity of this Precaution, and the infinite advantages to be derived from it, we need only refer to the Inftance of the Deficiencies in the laft War, and in the firft year of the Peace, as already mentioned *.

* Vide P. 18 to 21.

Confiderable

Confiderable facility is likewife obtained by the Act, in afcertaining, charging, and accounting for the Duties of Excife and Stamps, particularly the former; and the Accounts in all the public Offices are fimplified in fuch a manner as greatly to accelerate the furnifhing fuch Information as may exhibit, from time to time, a juft view of the fituation of the Country. ^{*Simplification of Accounts.*}

It is not, however, in this inftance alone, that the object of fimplifying Accounts has been attended to; thofe who have adverted to the Reports of the Committees of 1786 and 1791, will perceive that the Income and Expenditure of the Country are therein fo developed, as to make a Subject clear and intelligible to every one, which was before in general little underftood.

The Syftem which has been uniformly adopted, during the Period before us, in every inftance of Loans or Lotteries, by receiving Propofals publicly, and contracting with thofe who make the moft favourable ^{*Mode of making Loans.*}

Offers,

Offers, infures to the Public the borrowing
on the beft Terms that exifting Circumftances will permit, as well as the deriving
the greateft poffible advantage in aid of the
Revenue annually from Lotteries, fo long as
the Legiflature fhall judge it proper, to avail
itfelf of that Refource.

Act for au-
diting Pub-
lic Ac-
counts.

Loffes to an immenfe Amount had been
fuftained by the Public, from Perfons to
whom large Sums of Money had been iffued,
and who had not rendered any Account *:
A very

---

* The late Commiffioners of the Public Accounts ftate,
in their 8th Report, that £. 126,000,000, iffued to various
Public Accountants in 16 years, to October 1780, exclufive
of the unfettled Debt of Lord Holland, were unaccounted
for;—and in their 10th Report, that between 1746 and 1783
there were 664 Perfons, Sub-accountants for Army Services,
who remained accountable to the Public for the Sum of
£. 38,933,920;—of the latter, more than 150 have rendered
Accounts to the new Board of Commiffioners for taking and
ftating the Public Accounts, to the Amount of upwards of
£. 35,000,000; befides all the Accountants in the ordinary
courfe.—It is not however meant to fuggeft, that by much
the greater part of the Totals ftated by the late Commiffioners for Public Accounts, though not accounted for, were
not in a great proportion properly expended; the Fact pro-
bably

A very large Proportion of them had never been called upon; the few who were, with thofe who voluntarily tendered themfelves, paffed their Accounts for Millions, before a Deputy or Clerk, appointed by an Auditor, who always confidered his own Office as a Sinecure. To remedy this Evil, an act was paffed in 1785, for better examining and auditing the Public Accounts of the Kingdom ; fince which, they have been examined with attention and fcrupulous exactnefs *,

bably is, that they were fo: But on the other hand it is highly improper, that the whole fhould not have undergone a regular invefligation in due time; and it is inconteftably true, that large fums have been loft to the Public, from the Parties, who failed to account for the fame, having in fome inftances become infolvent; and in others, from their property having defcended in a manner not now to be traced, which in moft of the Cafes would render any Attempt, at this time, to recover the Balances due, perfectly defperate.

* Sums amounting in the whole to near £. 800,000 have been re-paid into the Exchequer by Accountants, or their Reprefentatives, between January 5, 1784, and January 5, 1793, arifing from the Invefligation of the new Board of Accounts, and of the Comptrollers of Army Accounts; including fome Balances re-paid by Agents in confequence of a ftrict Examination made by three Gentlemen appointed for that Purpofe.

and

and the effects of this law will be felt in its full extent, now that we are forced into a War, little expected when the firſt edition of this Examination was publiſhed laſt year. Sums, beyond all belief to Perſons not experienced in ſuch Matters, would have been ſaved, if ſuch an Inſtitution had been provided previous to the two laſt Wars.

It muſt be in the recollection of every one, how univerſal a perſuaſion prevailed, that the ſeparation of the American Colonies from Great Britain would be felt as a great and ſevere wound, injuring our Reſources and leſſening our Navigation. We cannot, therefore, but contemplate with ſome degree of Pleaſure on the Effects produced by the Meaſures before alluded to, and by various other Cauſes which have contributed to the general Proſperity of the Country. To compare the Revenue at different Periods, before and ſince the Separation, would not alone be admitted as a Criterion,

becauſe

becaufe new Taxes have been fince added
to a large Amount; although it is no equivocal Proof of the Energy of the Country,
that, under an immenfe accumulation of
Debt and Taxes, it has been able to effect
moft fuccefsfully what was never before
attempted, the gradual and certain reduction
of the Debt.

A more direct Argument will however
arife from an inquiry into the State of our
Navigation and Commerce during the Years
of our greateft profperity in the laft Peace,
and at this Time.—In this Inquiry there
occurs fome difficulty as to the Navigation;—it is to be lamented, that previous to
1786, no Ships were regiftered in Great
Britain, except thofe which traded to the
Plantations: Entries of Ships outwards were
till then made very loofely; there was no
fort of check on the Mafter or Owner, who
invariably reprefented the Veffels of a lefs
burthen than the real Tonnage, to fave the
payment of Light Duties and other charges;
notwithftanding which, a tolerable judgment

ment may be formed of the Increafe of our Navigation, by comparing the *Numbers* of the Ships cleared out at the different Periods, having in view that, previous to the feparation of the Colonies from Great Britain, all American Shipping was deemed Britifh, and that the Size of our Ships is now larger than at that Time.

Number

umber of Britifh Ships
UTWARDS from Great Britain.

* Shipage.	Ships.	Tonnage.
1772 - 7,6811	1789 - 13,648 -	1,515,021
1773 - 8,2042	1790 - 12,762 -	1,424,912
1774 - 8,5904	1791 - 13,501 -	1,511,246
1775† 9,2854	1792 - 13,881 -	1,560,307

£.17,821,000
19,130,000
19,669,000
19,629,000

the following Years:

— 11,498
— 12,059
— 12,536
— 12,931

	Foreigures.	Britifh Manufactures.	Total.
772	-£.00	-£.13,779,000	-£.19,340,000
773	- 00	- 14,921,000	- 20,120,000
774	- 00	- 16,810,000	- 22,731,000
775	- 00	- 18,310,000	- 24,878,000

* The propry large; but it is impoffible to afcertain the number
them, with a
† From this
‡ A comparods, becaufe, previous to the late Regifter Act, no
count was kept, as the fhips were not accurately meafured before
e paffing of the

H   In

oint of View as poſſible, the following
incipal Heads which have been enumerated, in
to.

Price of £. 3 per Cents Conſol.
April 30th 1793.

   - - £.77½

Price of India Stock.
April 30th 1793.

   - - £. 214

Value of Imports, 1792.

  - £. 19,629,000.

Value of Exports, 1792.

Foreign Produce.   *TOTAL.*

o £. 6,568,000   £. 24,878,000

o. of Britiſh Ships entered Inwards to
Great Britain in 1792.

   - - 13,030.

Britiſh Ships cleared Outwards from
Great Britain in 1792.

   - - 13,881.

iount of Permanent Taxes in 1792.

  - £. 14,284,000

n 1792 the whole of the Revenue,
xpenditure on the reduced Peace Eſtabliſhment.

   - £. 2,031,000 †

not paid till a ſubſequent Year.